J and R Lamb

Church Furnishers, Church Decorators

J and R Lamb

Church Furnishers, Church Decorators

ISBN/EAN: 9783743420809

Manufactured in Europe, USA, Canada, Australia, Japa

Cover: Foto ©Andreas Hilbeck / pixelio.de

Manufactured and distributed by brebook publishing software
(www.brebook.com)

J and R Lamb

Church Furnishers, Church Decorators

· J · & · R · LAMB ·

· 59 · CARMINE · STREET ·

SIXTH AVENUE CARS PASS THE DOOR.

· NEW · YORK ·

· CHURCH · FURNISHERS ·

· CHURCH · DECORATORS ·

THIS Catalogue is published as a supplement to our Metal Work Catalogue, Spring of '87, and will be found to contain a large number of new illustrations on various details of Church work—pulpits, lecterns, tablets, fonts, monuments, etc., etc. .   . . .

THIS is not intended to take the place of special designs, which we shall be pleased to make and submit for approval, upon receipt of information as to the article needed, position it is to be placed in, character and style of the building, and also a suggestion of the limitation of expenditure.

IF a design is desired for a large piece of work, as for example, pulpit, lectern, reredos, tomb, etc., a photograph of the position it is intended to occupy, will greatly aid us in arranging appropriate design.

PRICES of the various articles illustrated will be sent on request. Kindly give the page as well as the number.

ACH year we publish a revised edition of our various Catalogues, Metal Work, Wood Work, Stained Glass, Embroideries, Banners, Decoration and Monumental Work, but owing to the large number of new designs we have recently been making we find it necessary at this time to print a supplement to our Metal Catalogue. This will be found to give many points not covered by our catalogue of the early part of the year in regard to

Memorial Pulpits,

Eagle Lecterns,

Desk Lecterns,

Prayer-desks,

Altar Furniture,

Memorial Tablets, etc., etc.

Simple designs have been arranged to meet the requirements of many smaller parishes, and the expense will be found such as to permit of the use of metal work in many cases in place of wood.

Prices forwarded for any of these designs upon application. Photographs and sketches will be submitted upon receipt of the needed information as to article needed and position it is to occupy, and an approximate idea of desired expenditure.

PULPITS.

Examples of our various Designs for Memorial Pulpits can be seen in the following Churches :

Church of the Mediator,	11th Ave., New York City.
Central Baptist Church,	42d Street, " " "
St. James M. E. Church,	Madison Ave., " " "
St. Peter's Church,	20th Street, " " "
St. Luke's Church,	Hudson St., " " "
Holy Trinity Church,	Harlem, " " "
Tabernacle Baptist Church,	2d Ave., " " "
St. Ann's Church,	Brooklyn, N. Y.
St. Mark's Church,	" "
Bethany Pres. Church,	Morrisania, N. Y.
First Baptist Church,	Hoboken, N. J.
St. Joseph's Church,	Newark, N. J.
First Reformed Church,	New Brunswick, N. J.
Trinity Church,	Trenton, N. J.
Reformed Church,	Brookdale, N. J.
Grace Church,	Lockport, N. Y.
Bethesda Church,	Saratoga Springs, N. Y.
St. Paul's Cathedral,	Syracuse, N. Y.
Grace Church,	Utica, N. Y.
Christ Church,	Bordentown, N. J.
Christ Church,	Rochester, N. Y.
Trinity Church,	Buffalo, N. Y.
Trinity Church,	Elmira, N. Y.
St. John's Church,	Johnstown, N. Y.
St. Andrew's Church,	Philadelphia, Pa.
St. Luke's Church,	" "
Packer Memorial Church,	Mauch Chunk, Pa.
St. Michael's Church,	Birdsboro, Pa.
St. Luke's Church,	Altoona, Pa.
St. James' Church,	Fair Haven, Conn.
St. Andrew's Church,	Meriden, Conn.
St. Paul's School,	Concord, N. H.
Church of the Redeemer.	Lexington, Mass.
St. John's Church,	Saginaw, Mich.
Grace Church,	Chicago, Ill.
Baptist Church,	Cincinnati, Ohio.
St. James' Church,	Painesville, Ohio.
First Congregational Church,	Baltimore, Md.
Soldier's Home,	Richmond, Va.
Trinity Church,	Covington, Ky.
Church of the Good Shepherd,	Augusta, Ga.
St. Paul's Church,	Selma, Ala.
Trinity Church,	Gainesville, Fla.

J. & R. LAMB,   59 Carmine St., N. Y.

Nº 44

Nº 45

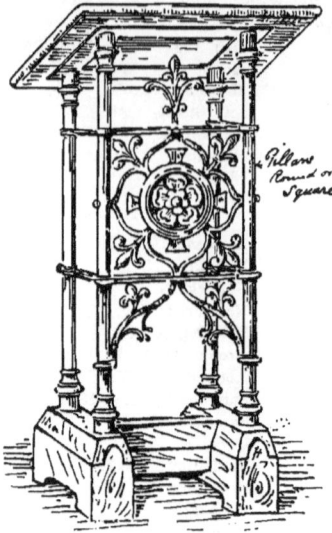

Pillars
Round or
Square

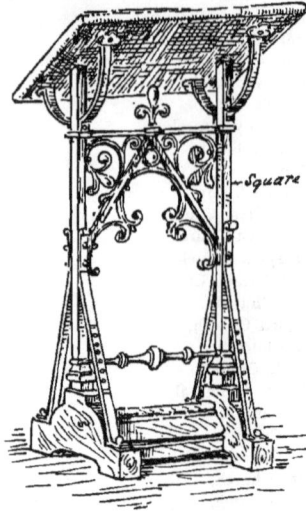

Square

-Nº 46-

-Nº 47-

Twisted

J. & R. Lamb,   59 Carmine St., N. Y.

Nº 96

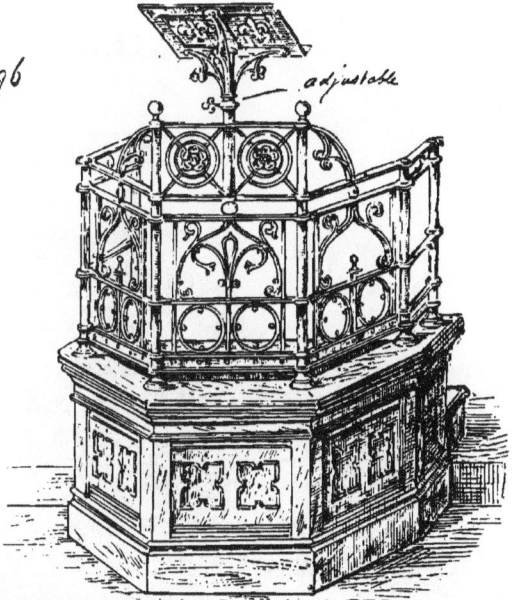

adjustable

Pulpits in
Brass & Oak

adjustable —

Nº 97

Pulpit in Polished Brass & Wood

No 1102

EAGLE LECTERNS.

Examples of our various Designs of Eagle Lecterns can be seen in the following Churches:

All Saints Church, .	Henry St., New York City.
Church of the Holy Spirit,	Madison Ave., " " "
Christ Church, . .	5th Ave., " " "
Orphan Asylum, .	5th Ave., " " "
St. Clement's Church, .	. . " " "
St. Peter's Church, .	20th St., " " "
St. Luke's Church,	Hudson St., " " "
St. Stephen's Church,	. . " " "
The Woman's Hospital,	49th St.& 4th Ave." " "
Christ Church, . .	Brooklyn, N. Y.
Church of the Atonement,	" "
Grace M. E. Church, .	" "
Herkimer St. Baptist Church,	" "
Holy Trinity Church, .	" "
St. Ann's Church,	" "
St. Stephen's Church,	" "
St. Ann's Church, .	Morrisania, N. Y.
Grace Church, .	Long Beach, L. I.
St. Mark's Church, ,	Islip, L. I.
Grace Church, . .	Jersey City, N. J.
First Presbyterian Church,	Newark, N. J.
Christ Church, . .	Hackensack, N. J.
St. Peter's Church,	Perth Amboy, N. J.
Christ Church, . . .	Woodbury, N. J.
Church of the Holy Communion,	Norwood, N. J.
Church of the Holy Comforter, .	Poughkeepsie, N. Y.
Zion Church, . . .	Dobbs Ferry, N. Y.
Grace Church,	Waterville, N. Y.
Trinity Church,	Lansingburgh, N. Y.
Trinity Church,	Elmira, N. Y.
St. James Church,	Fordham, N. Y.
Bethesda Church, . ,	Saratoga Springs, N. Y.
St. Barnabas Chapel,	Troy, N. Y.
St. Paul's Cathedral,	Syracuse, N. Y.
St. Paul's Church,	South Norwalk, Conn.
Christ Church, .	Waltham, Mass.
Church of the Redeemer,	Lexington, Mass.
Episcopal Church, .	Auburndale, Mass.
St. Stephen's Church,	Lynn, Mass.
St. Luke's Home, .	Roxbury, Mass.
St. Paul's Church,	Boston, Mass.
Trinity Church,	Lenox, Mass.

Church of the Epiphany,	Philadelphia, Pa.
St. Andrew's Church, .	" "
St. Mark's Church, .	Frankfort, Philadelphia, Pa.
Packer Memorial Church,	Mauch Chunk, Pa.
St. David's Church, .	Hanayunk, Pa.
Trinity Church, .	Williamsport, Pa.
St. Mary's Church, . .	So. Portsmouth, R. I.
Church of the Incarnation	Washington, D. C.
Church of the Redeemer.	Baltimore Md.
St. Barnabas' Church, .	" "
St. John's Church, .	Hagerstown, Md.
St. Paul's Church,	Richmond, Va.
Christ Church,	New Orleans, La.
Grace Church,	Anniston, Ala.
Christ Church,	Vicksburg, Miss.
St. Luke's Church,	San Francisco, Cal.
Christ Church, .	Ottawa, Ont.
St. Paul's Church,	Milwaukee, Wis.
St. Matthew's Church,	Kenosha, Wis.
Church of Our Saviour,	Cincinnati, Ohio.
St. Paul's Church, .	" "
St. James' Church,	Zanesville, Ohio.
St. James' Church, .	Painesville, Ohio.
St. John's Church,	Dubuque, Iowa.
Christ Church,	St. Paul, Minn.
St. Luke's Church,	Hastings, Minn.

The designs shown on pages 8 to 12 are Eagle Lecterns in which the conventional bird is used, similar to the Continental and English styles. For designs of naturalistic birds consult our general Metal Catalogue or write for photographs.

Pages 13 to 17 show various designs of Desk Lecterns, ranging from simple and inexpensive forms to more elaborate styles.

On page 18 are shown new designs for a combination of Lectern and Prayer-desk, an article of furniture which can be utilized for reading the Prayers from as well as the Lessons.

Pages 19 and 20 give designs of brass Pulpit-desks, which can be applied to wooden pulpits already in place; numbers 89 and 90 showing methods of lighting by gas and by pulpit lamps, with hooded shade to protect the minister's sight.

J. & R. LAMB,   59 Carmine St., N. Y.

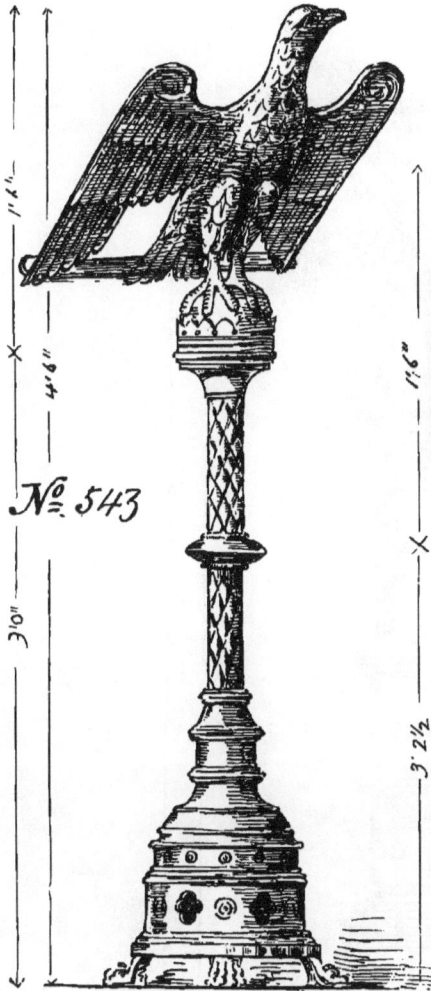

1' 4"

4' 6"

No. 543

3' 0"

1' 3"

Small Conventional
Eagle Lecterns

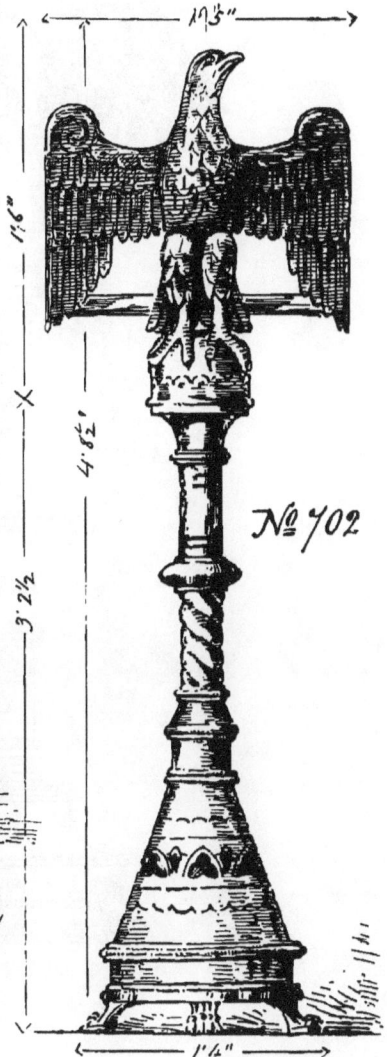

1' 5"

1' 6"

No. 702

4' 6½"

3' 2½"

1' 4"

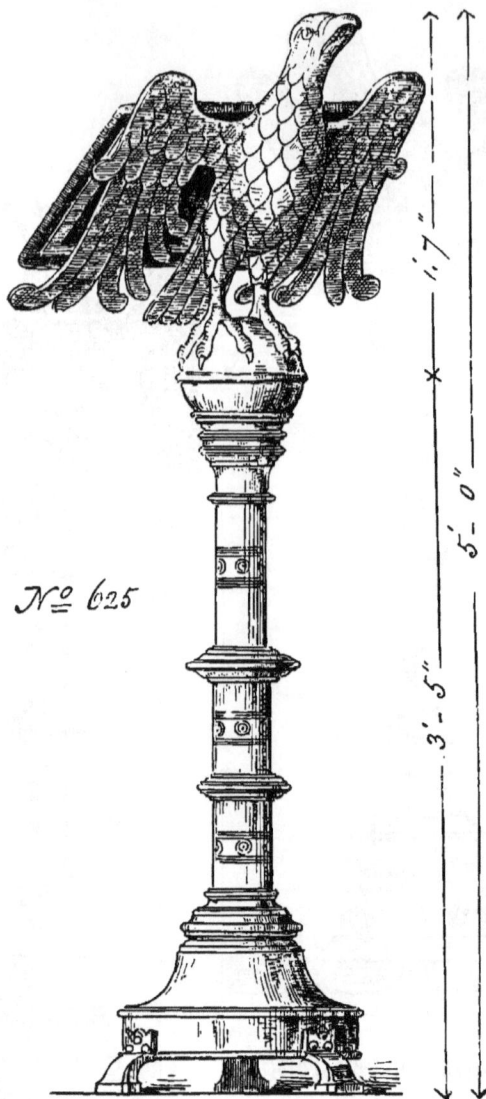

№ 625

5' - 0"

3' - 5"

1' - 7"

J. & R. LAMB,   59 Carmine St., N. Y.

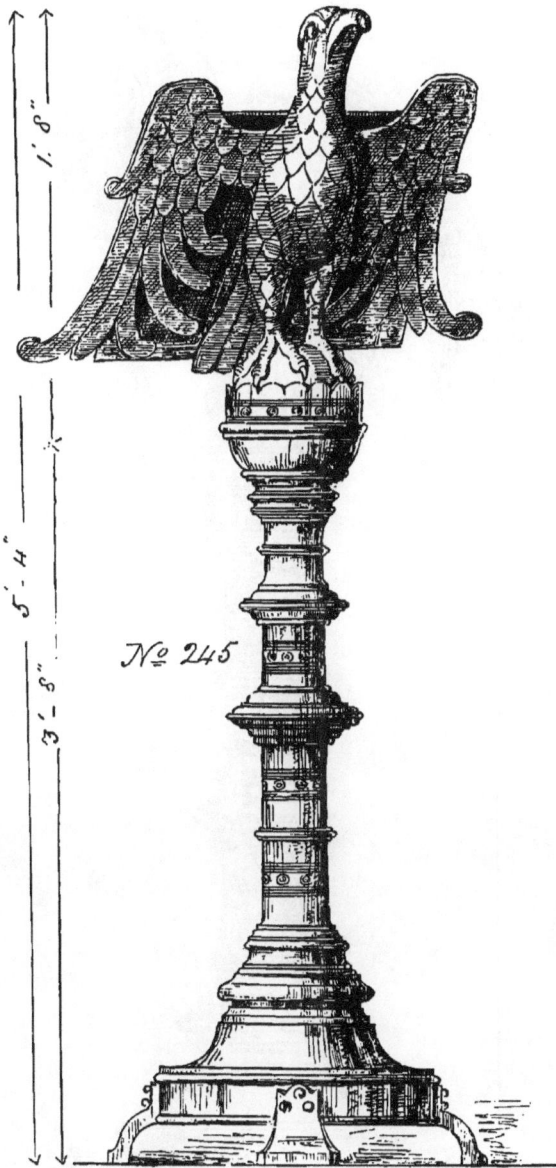

1' 8"

5' 4"

3' 8"

№ 245

J. & R. LAMB, 59 Carmine St., N. Y.

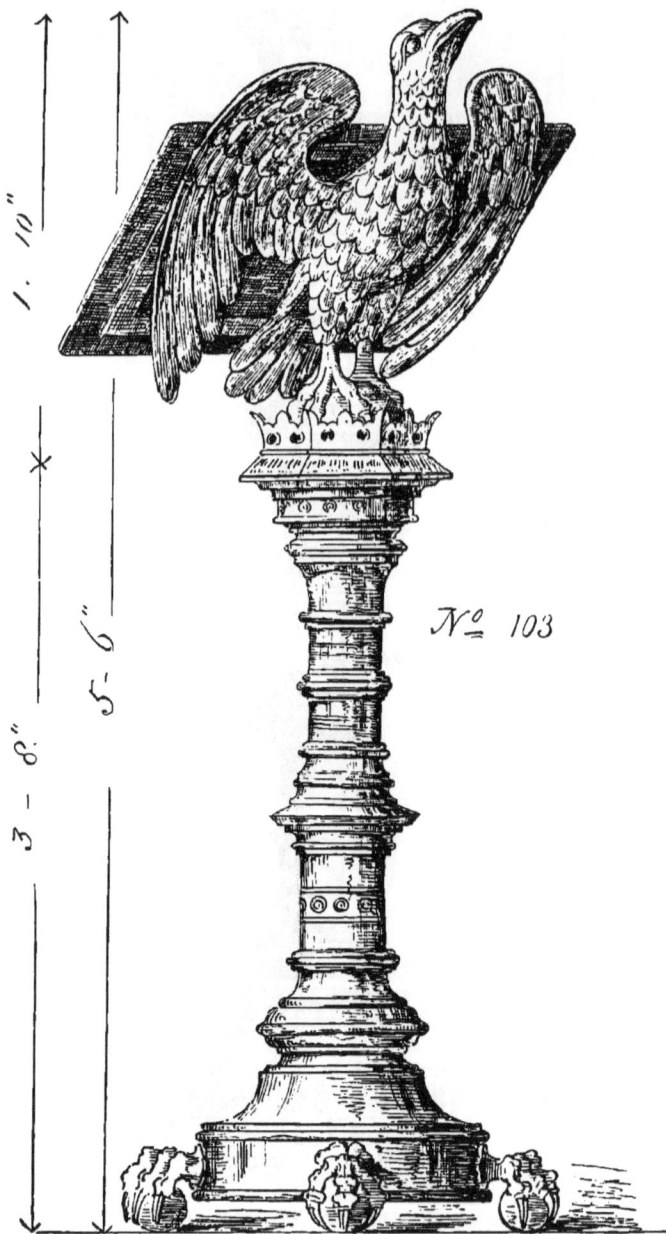

N° 103

1. 10"

3 - 8"

5 - 6"

J. & R. Lamb,   59 Carmine St., N. Y.

N° 71

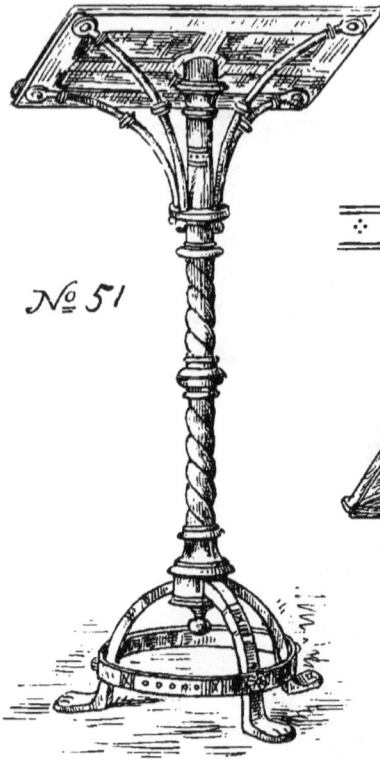

N° 51

☙ SIMPLE · LECTERNS

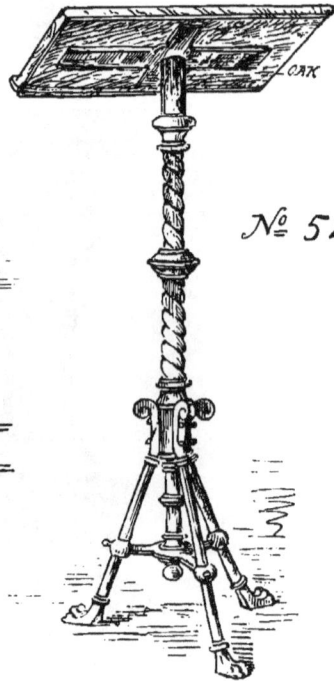

OAK

N° 52

IN POLISHED BRASS

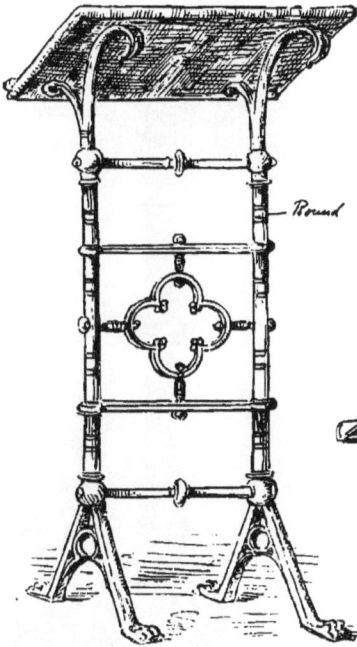

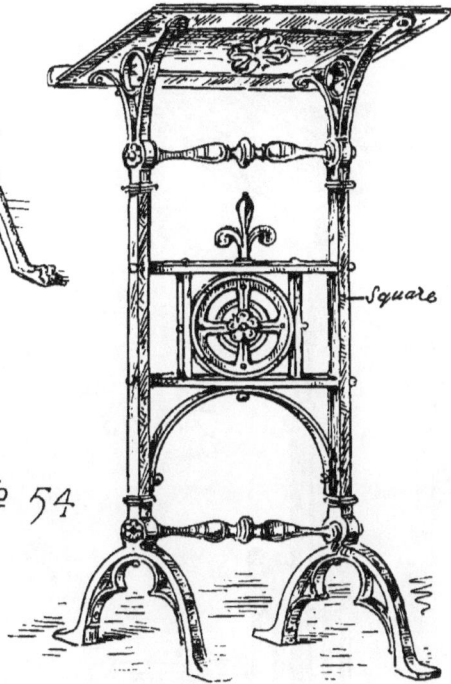

Lecterns in Polished Brass, or Brass & Iron

Round

Square

№ 53

№ 54

LECTERNS IN POLISHED BRASS

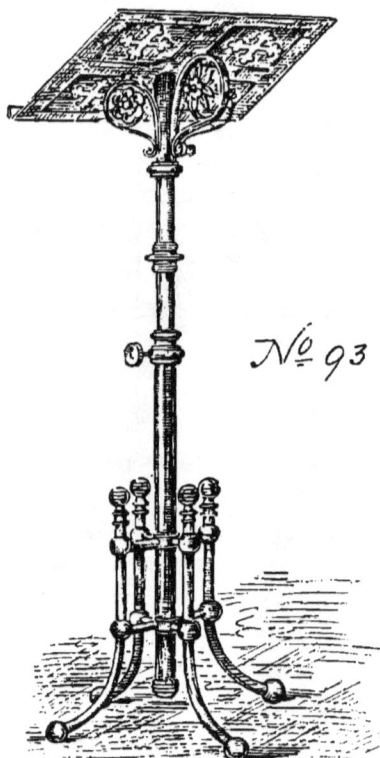

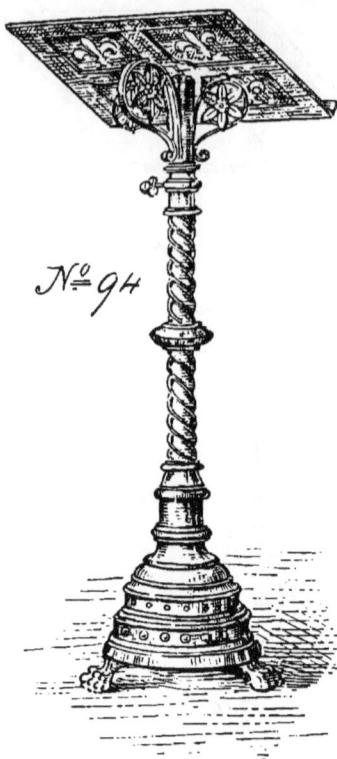

No 94

No 93

Plan of Base
of no 94

Scale ⅛ = to a foot

LECTERNS IN POLISHED BRASS

SCALE $\frac{7^{in}}{8}$ TO A FOOT

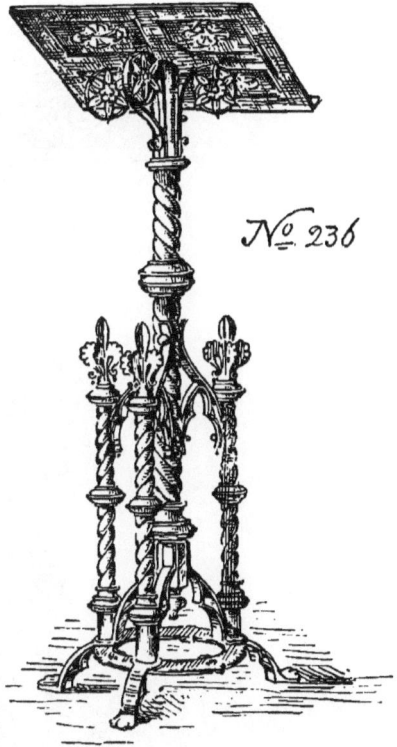

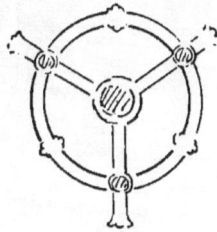

Nº 236

Nº 95

PLAN OF FOOT

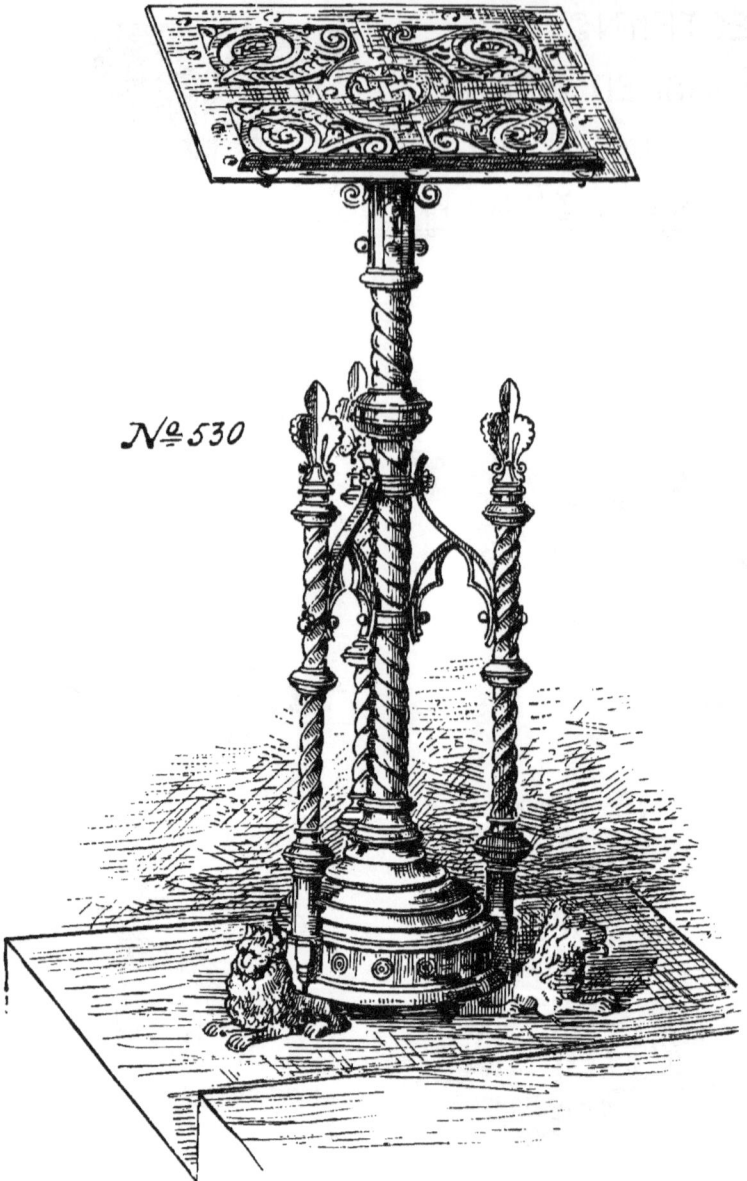

№ 530

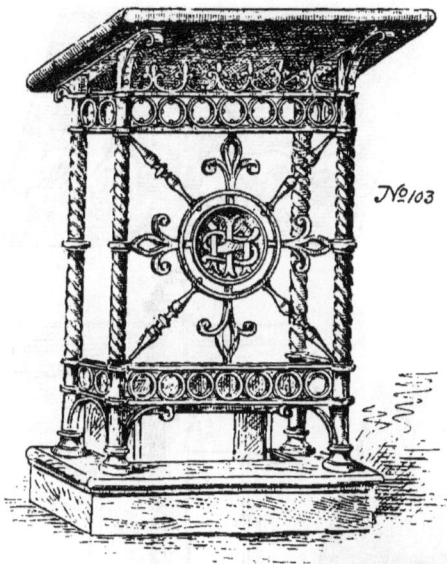

№ 103

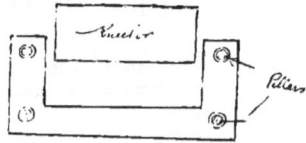

Kneeler

Pillars

Plan of Bases

№ 1137

PRAYER DESKS and
PULPIT DESKS COMBINED

in Polished Brass
and Wood

½in Scale

Pulpit Desks
in Polished Brass

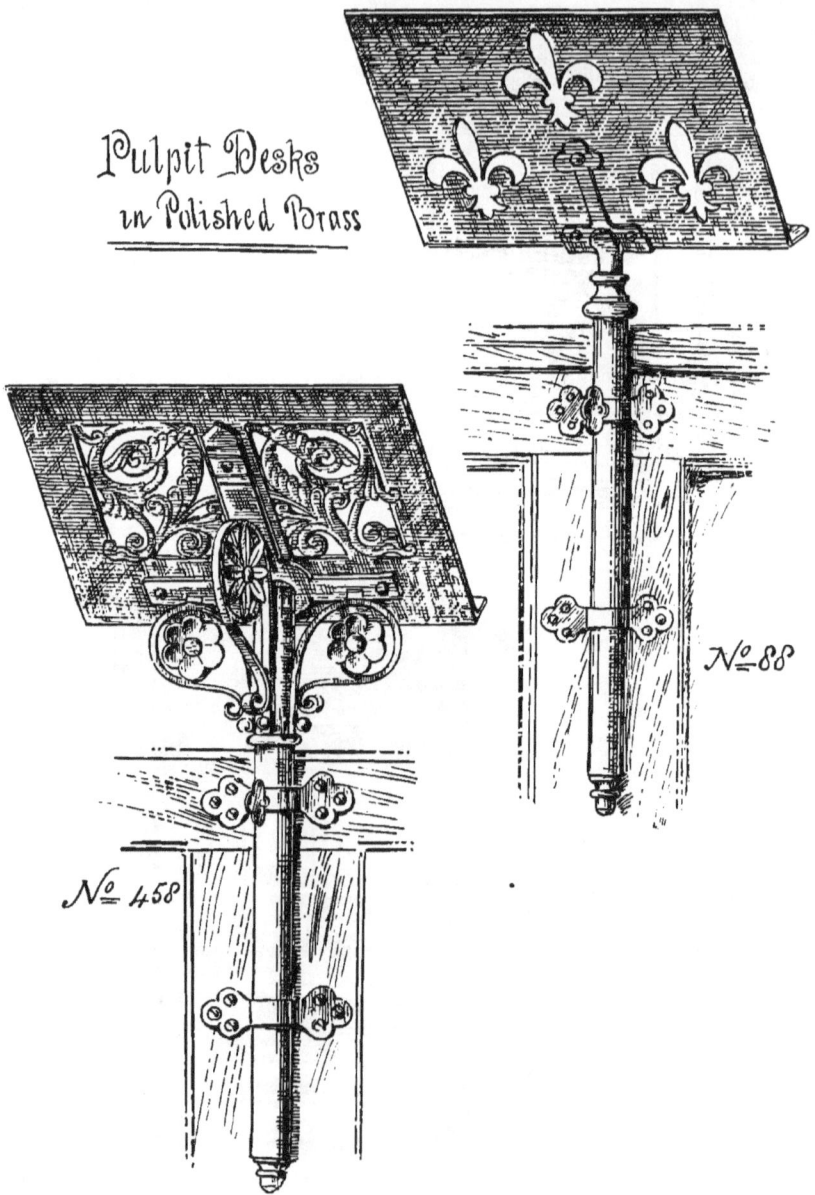

No 458

No 88

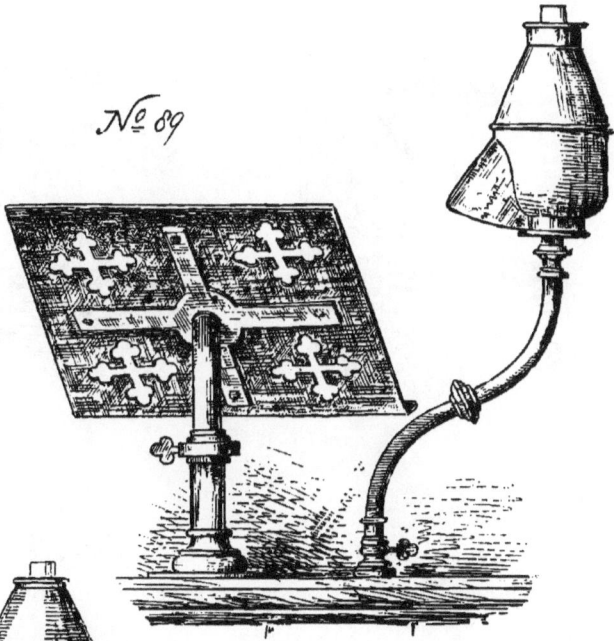

N⁰ 89

N⁰ 90

Manuscript Desks,
and Pulpit Light.

J. & R. LAMB,   52 Carmine St., N. Y.

Prayer and Litany Desks, in metal and wood, with plush or velvet book boards and kneeling cushions.

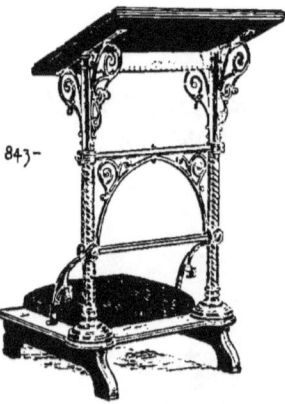
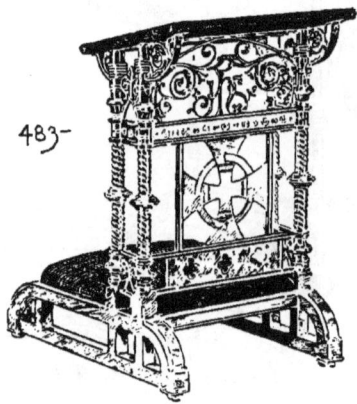

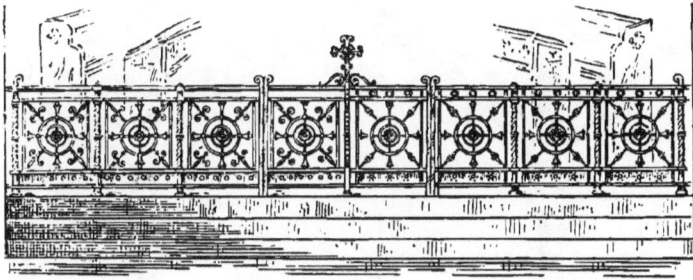

No. 43A   CHOIR – SCREEN   No. 43.B.

Choir Screen in polished or antique brass, bronze or wrought iron, or a combination of wood and metal as desired.

J. & R. Lamb,   59 Carmine St., N. Y.

No 1025

No 1008

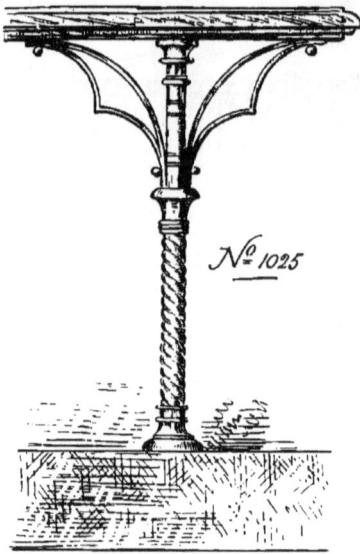

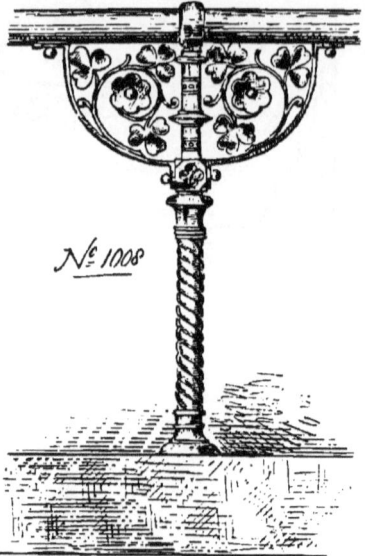

ALTAR RAIL STANDARDS

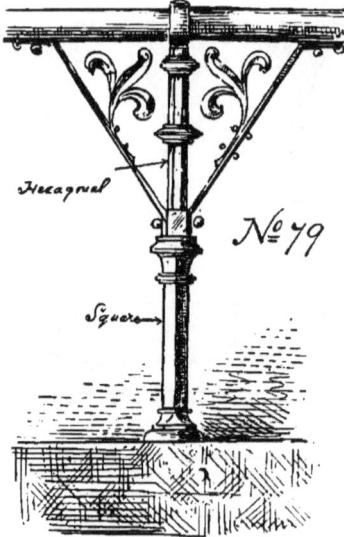

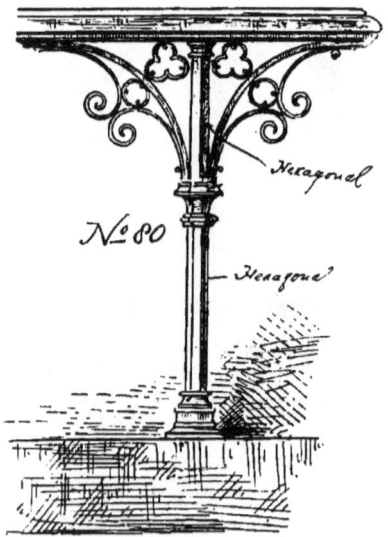

No 79

Hexagonal

Square

No 80

Hexagonal

Hexagonal

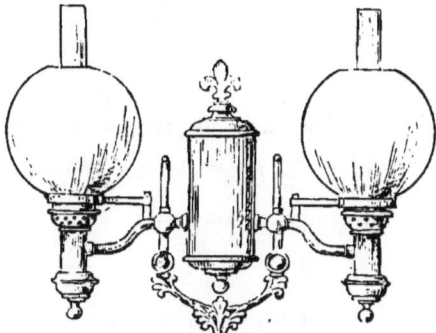

1094. A

1094 B

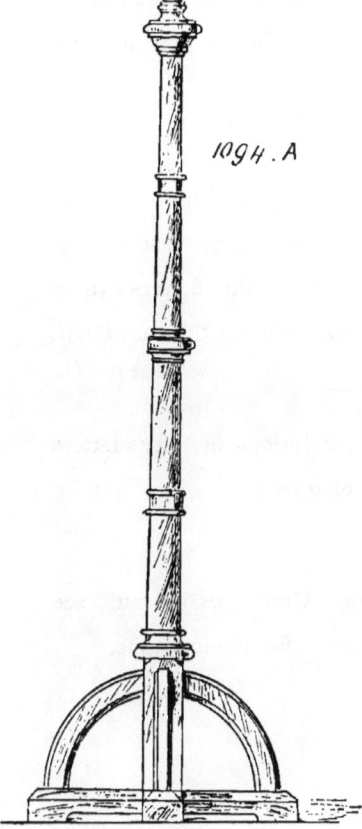
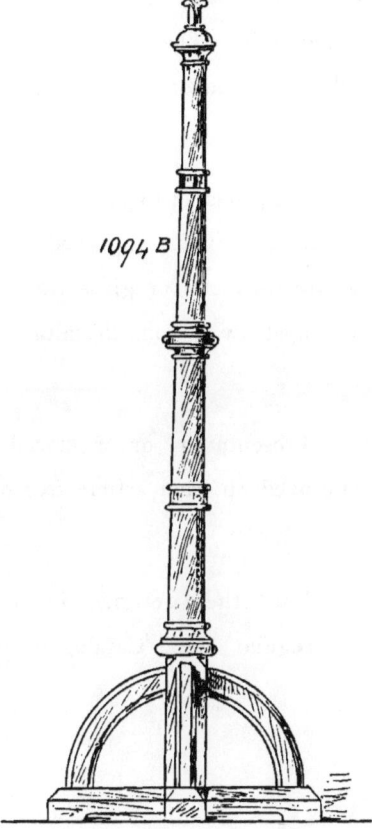

ALTAR FURNITURE.

On page 26 are designs for seven-light right and left branch Candlesticks, seven-light pyramidal form and five and three-light branches.

On pages 27 to 32 are shown various designs of Altar-desks, some with a single foot, and others with brackets on either side. The tops of some have pierced designs, and others are elaborately chased.

On pages 33 to 35 will be found designs of spun and cast metal Altar-vases, engraved and chased. Each vase is supplied with metal or glass lining in which the flowers can be arranged away from the altar without soiling the vase itself.

Presentation or memorial inscriptions of fifty letters engraved on each article free of charge.

For other designs, including Altar crosses, etc., see our regular Metal Catalogue, or send for photographs.

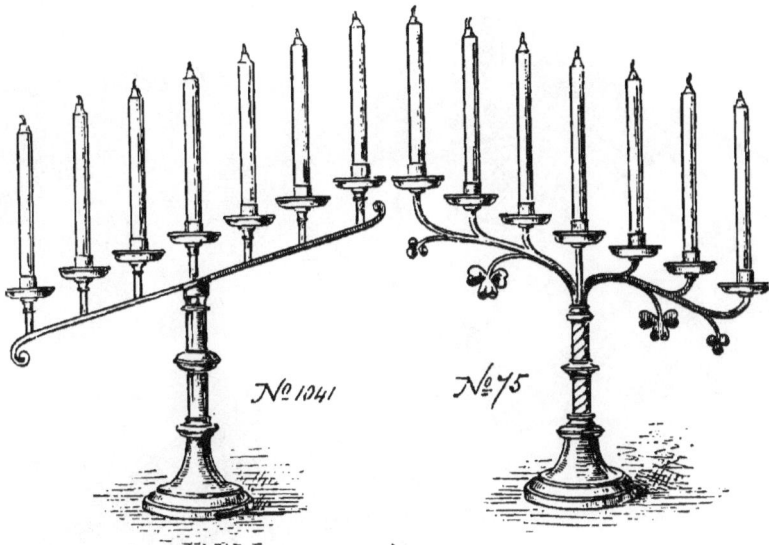

№ 1041   *№ 75*

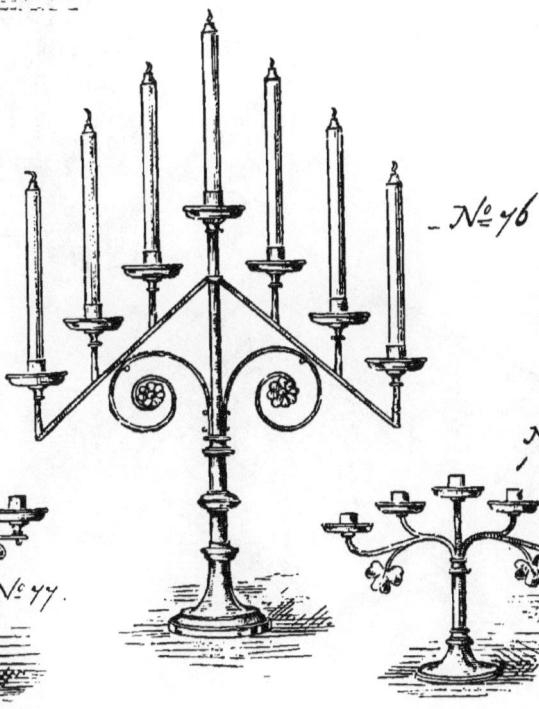

_ *№ 76*

№ 77.

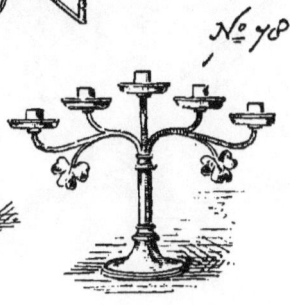

№ 78

_ № 68

№ 69 —

№ 70

No. 72

Altar Desks

No. 73

No. 74

No 65

No 66

No 67

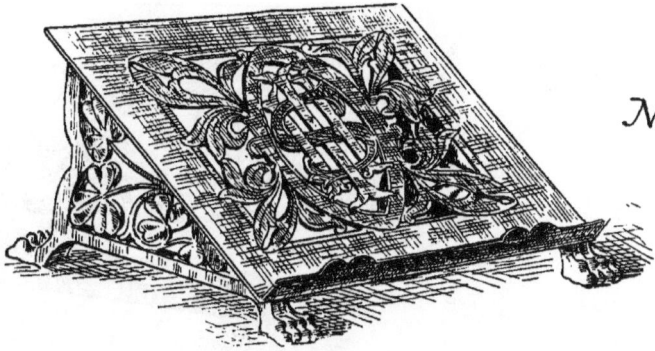

№ 59

№ 60

№ 61

№ 62

№ 63

№ 64

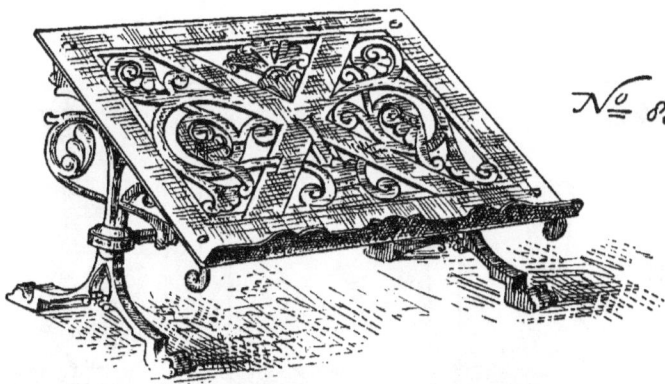

№ 85

№ 86

№ 87

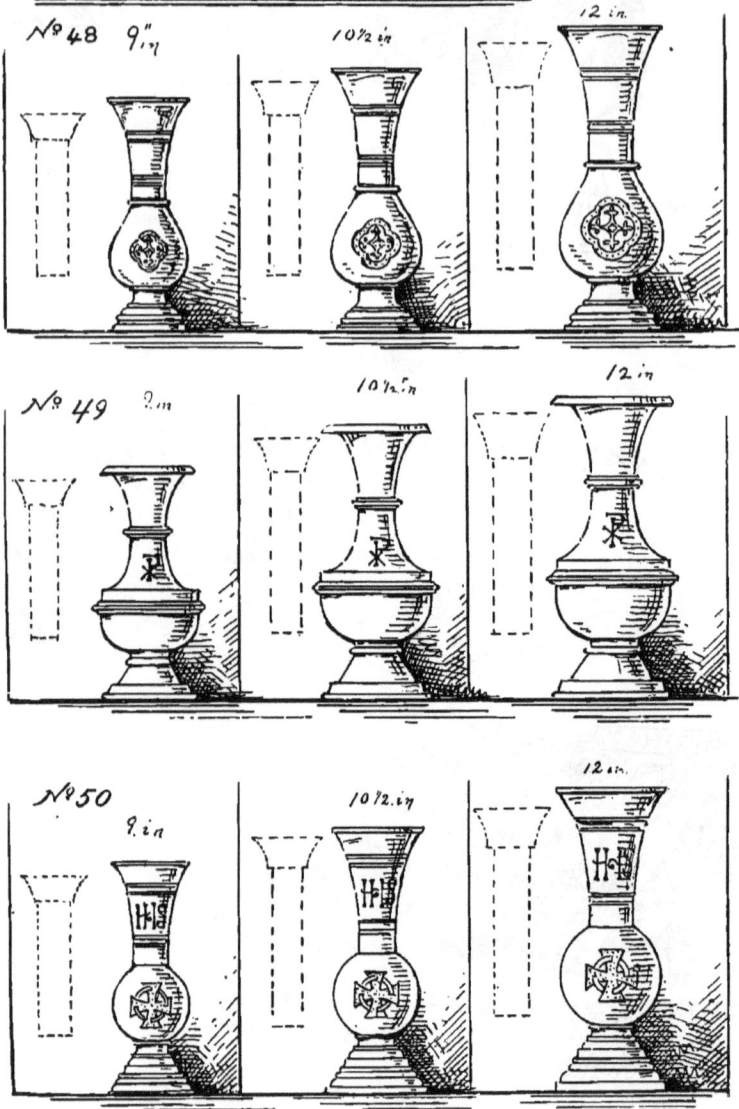

Nº 48 9″. 10½ in 12 in.

Nº 49 ? in 10½ in 12 in

Nº 50 9 in 10½ in 12 in.

DESIGNS FOR ALTAR VASES IN SPUN AND CAST METAL.

J. & R. LAMB, 59 Carmine St., N. Y.

№ 82
B

№ 82
A

№ 84
B

№ 84
A

DESIGNS FOR ALTAR VASES ENGRAVED AND CHASED.
J. & R. LAMB,   59 Carmine St., N. Y.

N⁰ 81
A

N⁰ 81
B

N⁰ 83
A

N⁰ 83
B

DESIGNS FOR ALTAR VASES ENGRAVED AND CHASED.
J. & R. LAMB,   59 Carmine St., N. Y.

BAPTISTRIES.

The construction and erection of the Font in the Baptistry of the Church, or in the situation which may be selected for it, necessarily admits of the greatest variety of taste, and the few examples which our limited space permits us to give can only be regarded as suggestions. The size, style and material of the Font itself, of the Font Ewer, the Standard Rail, etc., should all be considered with regard to the architecture of the Church, the amount of space at disposal, and the nature of the light. The fuller the information furnished us the greater will be our means of determining these vital points, and a sketch or a cut can be promptly forwarded that will meet the wants of the case. Whenever it is possible to dignify the rite of baptism by having a Baptistry designed for such services it is very much wiser so to do, and we shall take pleasure in making any suggestions and submitting plans designed to secure this result wherever the original plan of the church building did not include the idea of a Baptistry.

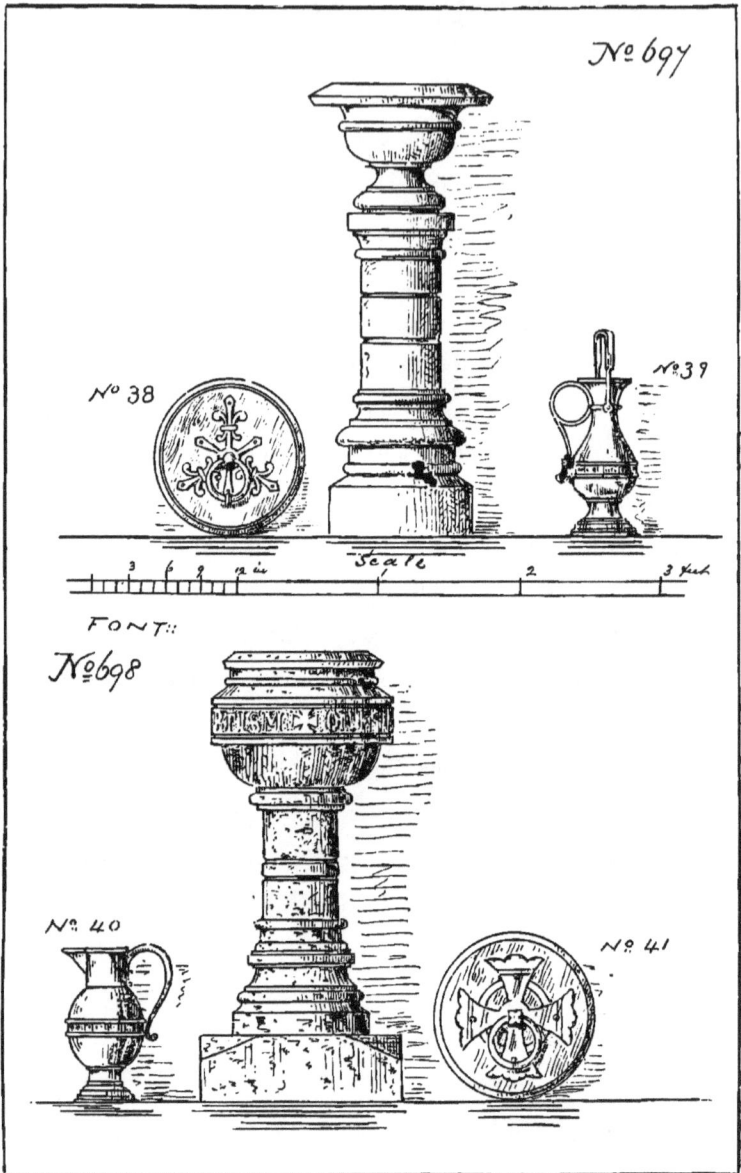

Nº 697

Nº 38

Nº 39

Scale

3   6   9   12 in   2   3 feet

FONT:

Nº 698

Nº 40

Nº 41

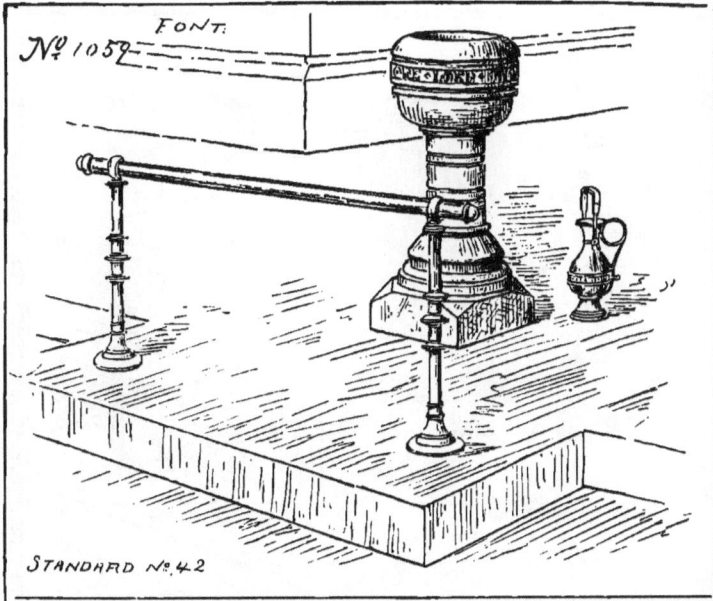

FONT.

Nᵒ 1059

STANDARD Nᵒ 42

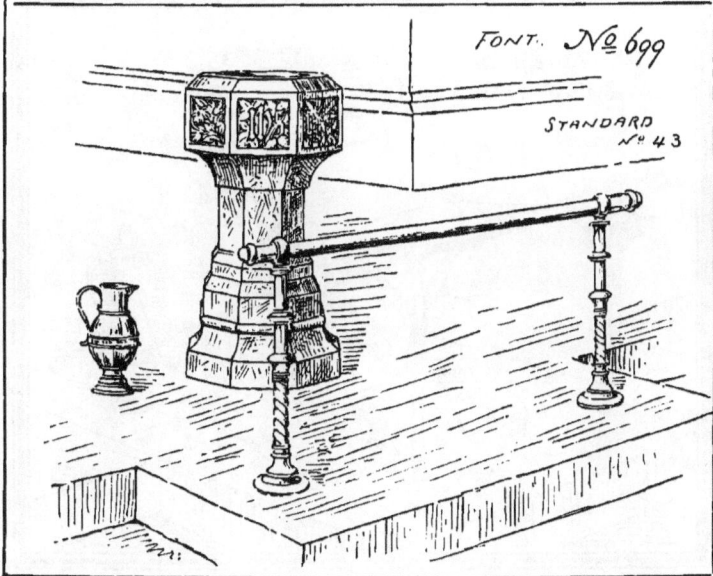

FONT. Nᵒ 699

STANDARD Nᵒ 43

-Font. 705-
-Standard -1005-
-Font ewer 777C-

-Font 624A-
-Standard 1025-
-Font ewer 777A-

No. 1079. A

No. 777
A

No. 777
B

No. 777
C

DESIGNS FOR FONT EWERS.

J. & R. LAMB.   59 Carmine St., N. Y.

Nº 98

Nº 99

Nº 100

Nº 1079 B

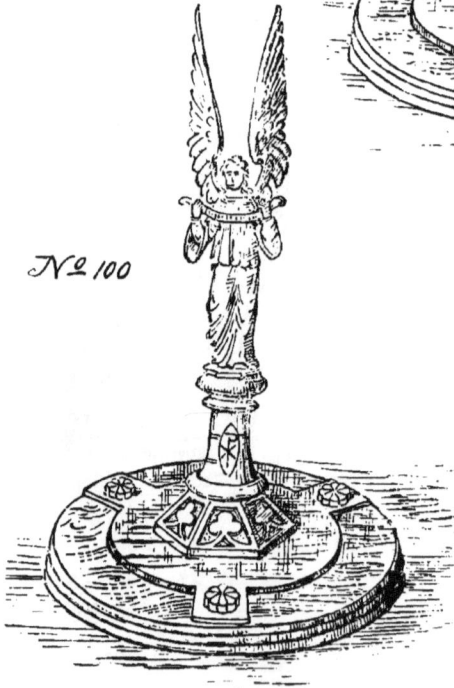

DESIGNS FOR FONT COVERS AND FONT BUCKETS.

J. & R. LAMB, 59 Carmine St., N. Y.

No 666

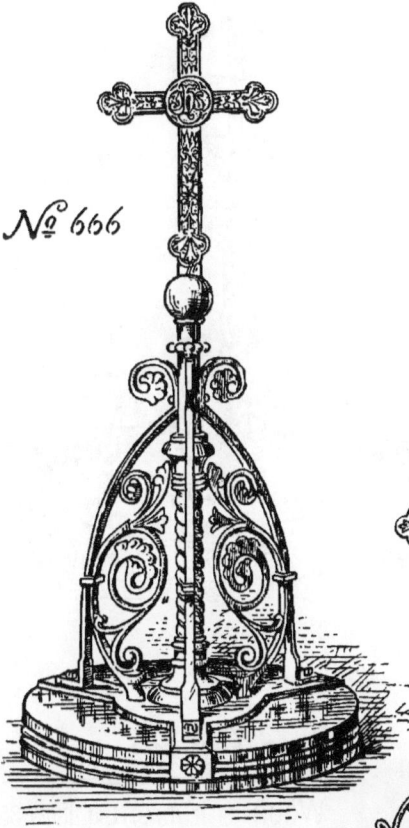

PLAN
(small scale

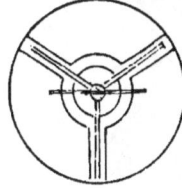

No 92

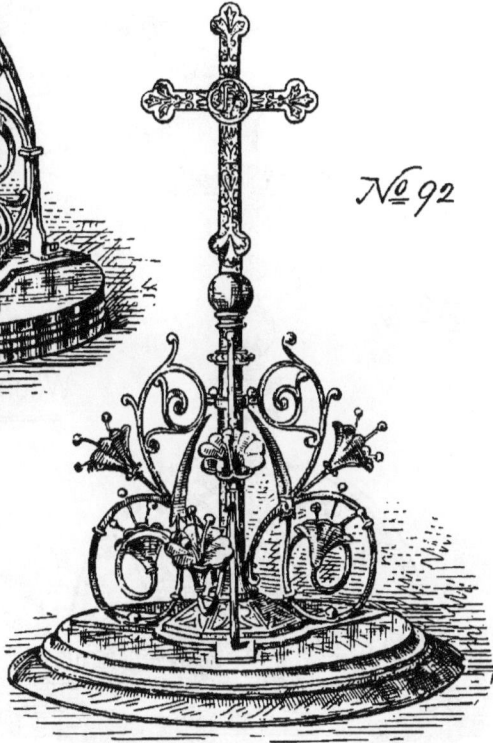

FONT COVERS
— IN —
POLISHED BRASS

J. & R. LAMB,   59 Carmine St., N. Y.

N⁰ 1079. C

FONT EWER

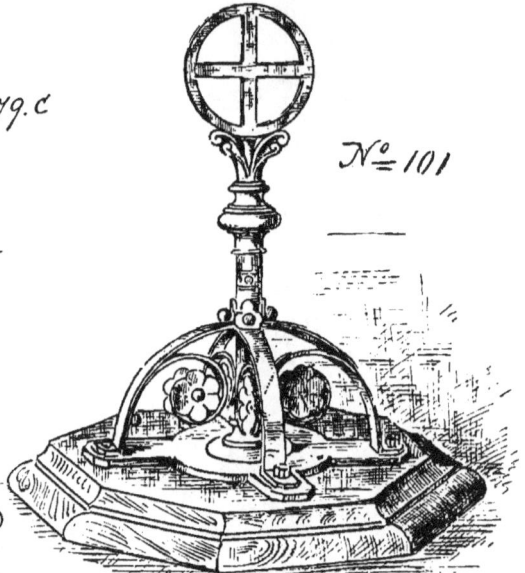

N⁰ 101

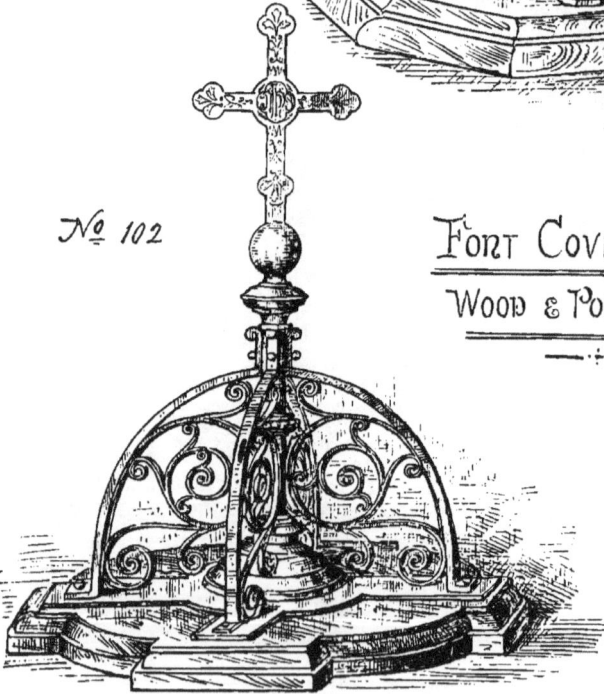

N⁰ 102

FONT COVERS IN
WOOD & POLISHED BRASS

Nº 91

PLAN
(Small Scale)

Nº 814

FONT COVERS
— IN —
BRASS POLISHED

COMMUNION
SERVICE
FIRST
PRESBYTERIAN
CHURCH
PATTERSON N.J.

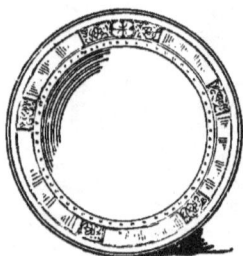

Designs and Photographs of Communion Silver, submitted by request.
Send for Illustrated Catalogue of SILVER WORK.

J. & R. LAMB,   59 Carmine St., N. Y.

45

The above cut shows the Ambler Memorial Tablet, which now hangs in the Corcoran Gallery at Washington, preparatory to being permanently placed in one of the governmental buildings there. This is a large bronze Tablet, modeled by Mr. Joseph Lauber, Sculptor, from a special design arranged by us at the suggestion of the committee. It commemorates the death of James Markham Ambler, the Surgeon in charge of the Jeannette Exploring Expedition, who was lost on the Lena Delta in the fall of 1881. The memorial was erected by his comrades, the Surgeons of the Navy, as a token of their esteem for him and regret at his untimely death. The correctness of the scene has been assured by the personal criticism of Engineer Melville, one of the survivors.

Above is shown the modeled Tablet of oxidized silver
erected in the room of the Eighth Company, Seventh Regi-
ment, New York, in memory of Henry C. Shumway and
George William Smith, late Captains of the Company. The
Tablet was made to fit into the panel above the mantel-
piece, which had previously remained undecorated. The
design for this was modeled by Mr. George T. Brewster
(pupil of Mércie, Paris). The panel receives in the centre
the figure of a Roman soldier with shield and sword. The
Regimental motto appears behind the figure, and a palm
branch deftly combines the several parts of the composition.

LOW RELIEF CENTRAL MEDALLION.—Jos. LAUBER, SCULPTOR, N. Y.

TO THE MEMORY OF
CHARLES FLINT PUTNAM
MASTER U S N WY
WHO VOLUNTEERED FOR DUTY ON BOARD THE
UNITED STATES STEAMER RODGERS A VESSEL
DESPATCHED TO THE ARCTIC OCEAN FOR THE RELIEF
OF THE JEANNETTE EXPLORING EXPEDITION

AFTER HAVING
GALLANTLY SECURED HIS SHIPWRECKED COMPANIONS
WHILE RETURNING TO HIS STATION AT CAPE
SERDZE KAMEN SIBERIA HE DRIFTED OFF TO SEA AND
PERISHED ALONE ON THE ICE IN SAINT LAWRENCE BAY
BEHRING STRAITS ABOUT JANUARY 31 1882

THIS : TABLET : WAS : ERECTED : IN
THE : NAVAL : ACADEMY : CHAPEL,
ANNAPOLIS : APRIL : 1886.

———

Other Tablets have been Executed by
us for the following College
Chapels and Buildings :

PRINCETON COLLEGE,
JOHNS HOPKINS UNIVERSITY,
LEHIGH UNIVERSITY,
TRINITY COLLEGE,
AMHERST COLLEGE,
RACINE COLLEGE,
THE U. S. NAVAL ACADEMY,
SETON HALL COLLEGE,
UNIVERSITY OF THE CITY OF NEW YORK,
NATIONAL DEAF MUTE COLLEGE,
    WASHINGTON, D. C.
DREW THEOLOGICAL SEMINARY,
LEHIGH UNIVERSITY,
WELLS COLLEGE,
UNION THEOLOGICAL SEMINARY, N. Y.,
RUTGERS' COLLEGE,
WASHINGTON AND LEE UNIVERSITY.

J. & R. LAMB,   59 Carmine St., N. Y.

48

GEORGE·BRINTON·MCLELLAN

MAJOR·GENERAL·U·S·A·
GOVERNOR·OF·NEW·JERSEY
ELDER·OF·THIS·CHURCH

OCTOBER·29·1885

I HAVE FOUGHT A GOOD FIGHT
I HAVE FINISHED MY COURSE
I HAVE KEPT THE FAITH

Nº 1110

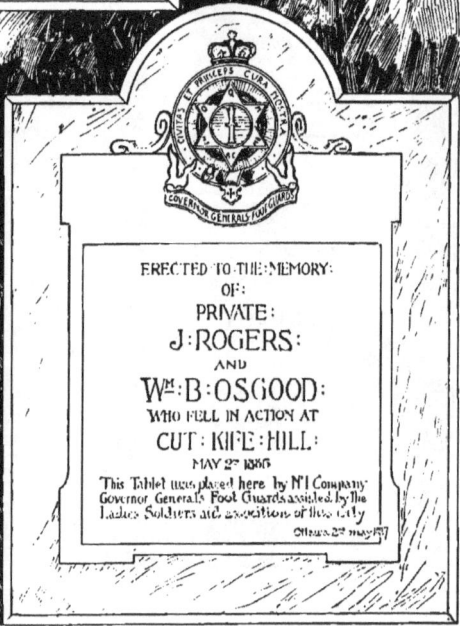

ERECTED·TO·THE·MEMORY·
OF·
PRIVATE·
J·ROGERS·
AND
Wᴹ·B·OSGOOD·
WHO FELL IN ACTION AT
CUT·KIFE·HILL·
MAY 2ᴰ 1885
This Tablet was placed here by Nº1 Company
Governor Generals Foot Guards assisted by The
Ladies Soldiers and exposition of this City
Ottawa 2ᵈ May 1887

THE EAST SIDE
⚜ LODGING HOUSE ⚜
FOR HOMELESS BOYS
ERECTED FOR
THE CHILDRENS AID SOCIETY
A·D·1880
BY
CATHERINE LORILLARD WOLFE

11.0
4.52"

A·D·1881 FOR THE EDUCATION AND
TRAINING OF ORPHAN·GIRLS
THIS COTTAGE IS ERECTED BY ⚜
MR AND MRS CORNELIUS VANDERBILT
+ IN·MEMORY·OF·THEIR·ELDEST·DAUGHTER
WHO·ENTERED·INTO·LIFE·ETERNAL·OCT·31 1873
IN·THE SIXTH YEAR OF HER·AGE·
He shall gather the lambs with his arms and shall carry them in his bosom.

J. & R. LAMB,   59 Carmine St., N. Y.

REV·EDWIN·F·HATFIELD·D·D

Nº912

FITCH SHEPARD
AND
DELIA MARIA DENNIS HIS WIFE

Nº913

REV·ELIHU·W·BALDWIN·D·D

Nº911

N° 955

IN MEMORY OF
MAX PIUTTI·
WHO DIED AUG 9TH 1885
AGED 32 YEARS
DIRECTOR·OF·MUSIC·AT·WELLS·COLLEGE
FROM·1875 TO 1884

N°926

AETERNAE MEMORIAE
CAROLI·HVRBANI·MORRIS·MA
COLLEGII·ORIELENSIS·OXON·OLIM·SOCII·
IN·HAC·ACADEMIA·
ER·X·ANNOS·
LITTERARVM·LATINARVM·GRAECARVMQVE·
PROFESSORIS·
QVI·OBIIT·SEXAGENARIVS·FERE·
VII·DIE·FEBRVARII·AD·MDCCCLXXXVI·
HOC·DESIDERII·PIETATISQVE·
MONVMENTVM·
DISCIPVLI·MAERENTES
F·C·

J. & R. LAMB,   59 Carmine St., N. Y.

No 878

THIS CHAPEL
ERECTED AD 1885
BY
CATHARINE LORILLARD WOLFE
OF THE CITY AND DIOCESE OF NEW YORK
IS MEMORIAL OF HER SISTER
MARY LORILLARD WOLFE
DAUGHTER OF
JOHN DAVID WOLFE
BY WHOM WAS ENDOWED THE
MARY WOLFE
PROFESSORSHIP OF ECCLESIASTICAL HISTORY

No 872

JAMES DANIELS SHEPPARD
BORN IN FROME ENG JAN 16 1793 DIED IN BUFFALO
OCT 24 1851 HE BEQUEATHED BY HIS LAST
WILL AND TESTAMENT TO THE VESTRY OF TRINITY
CHURCH THE SUM OF ONE THOUSAND DOLLARS TO
BE HELD IN TRUST THE INTEREST TO BE PAID BETWEEN
ST THOMAS DAY AND CHRISTMAS DAY IN EACH YEAR
TO NOT LESS THAN TEN INDIGENT PERSONS

J. & R. LAMB,   59 Carmine St., N. Y.

☩ York · Collegiate · Institute ☩
Built by Samuel Small AD 1371

In memory of
CHARLES T HOWARD
A MUNIFICENT BENEFACTOR OF
THIS INSTITUTION · ▦ · ☩ · ▦ · ☩ · ▦
Erected A D 1887

Nº 1062

Nº 1063

Nº 927

THE
CHRISTIANA · MASON · GIBSON
MEMORIAL · SCHOLARSHIP
OF THIS SCHOOL

MONUMENTS.

The question of monumental work is one in which, of late years, we have taken especial interest. Many of our clients, wishing to obtain designs which would be appropriate, and which would convey an idea of the character of the person in whose memory the monument was to be placed, have applied to us to solve the problem for them.

In all cases we have taken pains to secure in our work those points which to us, seem the most important: Durability, Individuality, and Artistic Unity. These can always be secured, even in the simplest work, if the designer, knowing the position the monument is to occupy, and having an approximate idea of the expense to be incurred, bases his design upon such knowledge.

Special designs will be submitted upon request, as well as photographs of work already executed.

CORRESPONDENCE SOLICITED.

MONUMENTS at WASHINGTON CONN.

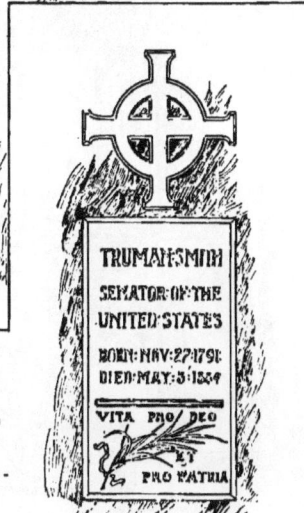

LINCOLN S GOLD
Son of
CORNELIUS B
and
MARGARET SWAN GOLD

JOB SWIFT GOLD

CATHARINE D GOLD
wife of
JOB SWIFT GOLD

TRUMAN SMITH
SENATOR OF THE
UNITED STATES
BORN NOV 27 1791
DIED MAY 3 1884

VITA PRO DEO

PRO PATRIA

MONUMENT at STAMFORD CONN.

DESIGN FOR PRIVATE ORATORY.
SPECIAL SKETCHES SUBMITTED UPON REQUEST.

J. & R. LAMB,   59 Carmine St., N. Y.

Zweybrückische Feyer

Der zu Mannheim den 17 Jenner dieses Jahrs geschehenen
Höchstbeglückten

Kurfürstlich Sächsischen

und

Pfalzgräulich Zweybrückischen
Vermählung

welche auf den 17 Merz in der Fürstlichen Schule in unterthänigst
treuer Ehrfurcht ankündigt

und zugleich
Von Vermählungen
Herzoglich Fränkischer und Rheinpfalzgräulicher
Erbprinzeßinnen mit auswärtigen Fürsten

als einem Grund ihrer Nachfolge in die Rheinpfälzische Lande, auf
erfolgten gänzlichen Abgang des Mannsstamms

Der Rector
Georg Christian Crollius/

Pfalzgräulich Zweybrückischer Historiographus und Bibliothekarius, in der Fürst-
lichen Schule Professor der Beredsamkeit und Geschichte, der Kur-
Bayerischen, Kurpfälzischen und Göttingischen historischen
Akademien rc. Mitglied.

Zweybrücken/ gedruckt bey Peter Hallanzy, Hochfürstl. Pfalz-
Zweybr. Hof- und Canzley Buchdrucker, 1769.

Tunc nova lux in Saxonia ortā eft, pacis videlicet iucun-
ditas —— Benedictae hac nuptiae, & eadem foemina bene-
dicta inter mulieres , & benedictus fructus ventris eius,
quia in ipfius copula terris fociata eft pax & laetitia.

Arnoldus Abbas Lubecenfis
in narratione de matrimonio Henrici pulchri,
Saxoniae Principis, & Agnens Palatinae Rheni,
Chron. Slav. L. IV, *cap. XX, ad an.* 1193.

Georg Christian Crollius

Zweibrückische Feier der zu Mannheim den 17 Jenner dieses Jahres geschehenen höchstbeglückten kurfürstlich sächsischen und pfalzgrävlich Zweyirückischen Vermählung

ISBN/EAN: 9783743624016

Hergestellt in Europa, USA, Kanada, Australien, Japan

Cover: Foto ©Andreas Hilbeck / pixelio.de

Weitere Bücher finden Sie auf **www.hansebooks.com**